Our American Family™

I Am
Irish
American

Ellwood Connor

The Rosen Publishing Group's
PowerKids Press™
New York

To Len—the best friend an author ever had.

Published in 1997 by The Rosen Publishing Group, Inc.
29 East 21st Street, New York, NY 10010

First Edition

Book Design: Erin McKenna

Photo Credits: cover © Joe Willis/International Stock; p. 4 © Arthur Tilley/FPG International Corp.; p. 7 © E. Nagele/FPG Internaitonal Corp.; p. 8 © Keystone View Co./FPG International Corp.; p. 11 © Jeffrey Katz/FPG International Corp.; p. 12 © Inc Pix/FPG International Corp.; p. 15 © Robert Stottlemyer/International Stock; p. 16 © Elliot Varner Smith/International Stock; p. 19 © Spencer Jones/FPG International Corp.; p. 20 © J. Zalon/FPG International Corp.

Connor, Ellwood.
    I am Irish American/ by Ellwood Connor.
        p.   cm. — (Our American family)
    Includes index.
    Summary: Discusses an Irish American's heritage, including famous Irish Americans
     and information about Ireland.
    ISBN 0-8239-5005-0
    1. Irish Americans—Juvenile literature. [1. Irish Americans.]
    I. Title. II. Series.
E184.I6T87 1997
973'.049162—dc21   96-53128
                                                                         CIP
                                                                          AC

Manufactured in the United States of America

Contents

My Family

My name is Maureen. I live in Detroit, Michigan. My grandparents came from the Republic of Ireland. In Ireland they were poor and had few opportunities. So, like many other Irish people, they came to the United States to find a better way of life.

My **relatives** (REL-uh-tivz) live near us in Detroit and in other nearby towns. I have lots of aunts, uncles, and cousins.

◀ I have learned a lot about being Irish American from my family.

Ireland

Ireland is an island next to the country of England. Many people call Ireland the **Emerald Isle** (EM-rald EYEL) because it has a lot of green grass. The grasslands are perfect for cows and sheep to **graze** (GRAYZ).

Ireland also has 800 lakes and rivers. The largest river is the River Shannon. There are many cities too. Dublin is the capital and largest city in Ireland. Cork, Galway, and Limerick are other major cities in Ireland.

Ireland is so green because it rains up to thirty inches a year. ▶

A National Hero

In school I learned about a man named Charles Stewart Parnell. He was an Irish leader in the 1800s. He worked hard to stop rich landlords from making the poor **peasants** (PEZ-unts) pay rent for their land. Charles was put in jail because of his beliefs, but the peasants still believed in him.

During this time, Ireland was ruled by England. But the Irish wanted to rule themselves. Charles supported this idea, which was called Home Rule. He was very important in Ireland's fight for **independence** (in-dee-PEN-dents).

◄ Charles Stewart Parnell led groups of people against Irish land laws.

The Potato Famine

Because of Ireland's rocky soil, potatoes were one of the few crops that could grow there. But in 1845 a plant disease attacked the potato plants. Almost all of Ireland's potato crops died, which caused a **famine** (FAM-in).

Many people did not want to leave their homeland, but they had to. More than 1.5 million people packed their belongings and left for the United States. Some of my **ancestors** (AN-ses-terz) came to the United States at this time.

Many Irish people had little to eat during the famine. Thousands died from starvation and disease. ▶

An Irish American President

In 1960 John F. Kennedy was elected President of the United States. He was the first Irish American to be elected. President Kennedy worked hard to improve working conditions and **civil rights** (SIH-vul RYTS) for all Americans. He **inspired** (in-SPYRD) many people and was very popular. My parents and many other Irish Americans were proud of Kennedy's **heritage** (HEHR-ih-tij). But in 1963, President Kennedy was killed by somebody who did not agree with his ideas.

◀ John F. Kennedy is known as one of the most popular presidents in history.

13

St. Patrick's Day

Saint Patrick was a religious leader and teacher who lived in Ireland hundreds of years ago. He taught the Irish people about Christianity. By the time Saint Patrick died on March 17, 461, he had spread Christianity throughout Ireland.

The date of Saint Patrick's death is a national holiday in Ireland and the United States. People wear green ribbons and clothes with **shamrocks** (SHAM-roks) to honor this day. St. Patrick's Day is my favorite holiday.

St. Patrick's Day is celebrated with ▶ parades all over the country.

The Great Irish Fair

Every September, more than one million people go to Coney Island in Brooklyn, New York, to celebrate the Great Irish Fair. Families walk along the Coney Island boardwalk. Bands play Irish music and Irish folksingers perform their songs. Irish athletes **compete** (kum-PEET) in special Irish sports, such as **hurling** (HER-ling). A beautiful, talented Irish girl is chosen to be Colleen Queen.

My family went to the Great Irish Fair a few years ago. I hope we can go again soon!

◀ Some Irish American girls display their heritage through traditional Irish dancing.

17

Food

On Sundays, my aunts, uncles, and cousins come to my house for dinner. I like to help my dad cook Irish food for the meal. Sometimes we make corned beef and cabbage. On other days we cook lamb stew. Lamb stew is cooked for a very long time in broth with potatoes, onions, and carrots. My mom bakes Irish soda bread with lots of raisins. Irish food is very delicious and filling.

Corned beef and cabbage is an Irish American meal that is eaten all over the United States. ▶

The Blarney Stone

There is a castle in Ireland called Blarney Castle. It was built in the 1400s. In one wall of the castle there is a stone that is known as the Blarney Stone. An Irish legend says that if you kiss the Blarney Stone, you will be given the gift of **persuasion** (per-SWAY-zhun). This means that you will be able to convince people to do things that you want them to do. When I am older, I would like to visit Ireland. When I do, I will kiss the Blarney Stone and see if the legend is true!

◀ To kiss the Blarney Stone you have to lie down and tilt your head backward!

21

Famous Irish Americans

When the first Irish people came to the United States, they had trouble finding jobs. People did not want to hire them because they were Irish. This was unfair. But even though things started out hard, many Irish Americans have succeeded. Rosie O'Donnell is a successful actress and talk show host. Bill Clinton was elected president of the United States twice. Sandra Day O'Connor was the first woman appointed to the Supreme Court.

I am proud to be Irish American.

Glossary

ancestor (AN-ses-ter) A person in your family who lived before you.

civil rights (SIH-vul RYTS) The rights of citizens, regardless of their race, age, religion, or sex.

compete (kum-PEET) To try to win at something.

Emerald Isle (EM-rald EYEL) A nickname for Ireland.

famine (FAM-in) A period of time when food is hard to find.

graze (GRAYZ) When animals eat grass and weeds.

heritage (HEHR-ih-tij) Cultural traditions that are handed down from parent to child.

hurling (HER-ling) A sport like field hockey that is played with fifteen people on each team.

independent (in-dee-PEN-dent) When a country rules itself.

inspire (in-SPYR) To fill with excitement about something.

peasant (PEZ-unt) A farmer of the lower class.

persuasion (per-SWAY-zhun) Being able to urge and convince someone of something.

relative (REL-uh-tiv) A member of a family.

shamrock (SHAM-rok) A leaf with three or four parts. Shamrocks are the national symbol of Ireland.

Index